CHRISTMAS DECORATIONS KIDS CAN MAKE

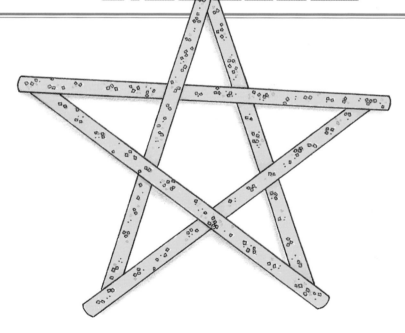

By Kathy Ross
Illustrated by Sharon Lane Holm

The Millbrook Press   Brookfield, Connecticut

*For Allison and Elm—wishing you a lifetime
of happy Christmases together.*—K. R.

For Heather Nicole—welcome little one!— S. L. H.

Library of Congress Cataloging-in-Publication Data
Ross, Katharine Reynolds, 1948-
Christmas decorations kids can make / by Kathy Ross ;
 illustrated by Sharon Lane Holm.
p. cm.
Summary: Provides step-by-step instructions for creating
thirty Christmas decorations, including a Santa tissue box,
foil angel, glistening snowman, table manger, and tube reindeer.
ISBN 0-7613-1565-9 (lib. bdg.) — ISBN 0-7613-1275-7 (pbk.)
1. Christmas decorations—Juvenile literature. 2. Handicraft—Juvenile
literature. [1. Christmas decorations. 2. Handicraft.]
I. Holm, Sharon Lane, ill. II. Title.
TT900.594'12—dc21
99-11938 CIP

Published by The Millbrook Press, Inc.
2 Old New Milford Road
Brookfield, CT 06804

Visit us on our Web site:http://www.millbrookpress.com

Library 5 4 3 2
Paper   5 4 3 2

Contents

CHRISTMAS DECORATIONS
KIDS CAN MAKE

Bow Tree

Last year's package bows can be turned into a charming decoration for this year.

What you need:

twelve pre-made package bows in various sizes and colors

green poster board (or you can paint white poster board green)

white glue

scissors

pencil

white rickrack

green yarn

hole punch

red felt scrap

What you do:

1 Arrange the bows on the poster board in the triangle shape of a Christmas tree. Use the larger bows along the bottom of the tree. Glue the bows in place. Let the glue dry before continuing.

2 Use the pencil to draw the outline of the tree around the bows. Add a trunk to the bottom of the tree. Cut out the tree.

3 Cut a pretty base for the bottom of the tree from the red felt. Glue the base over the trunk of the tree. Decorate the base with rickrack.

4 Cut a 6-inch (15-cm) piece of yarn to make a hanger for the tree. Punch a hole through the top of the tree. Thread one end of the yarn through the hole and tie the two ends together.

If you have a very large supply of bows, you might want to try making a bigger tree.

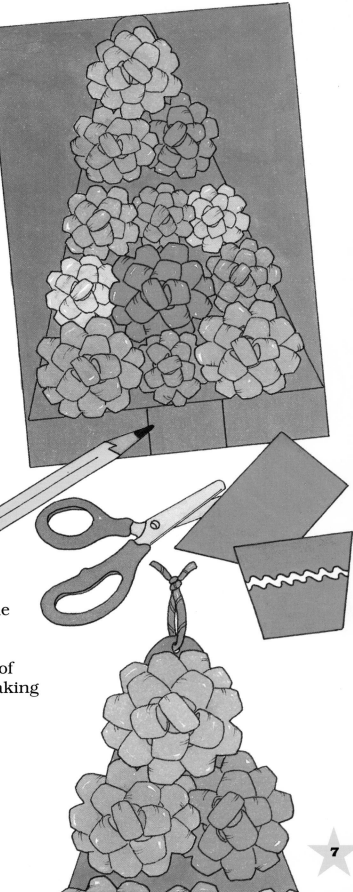

Stick Wreath

This sturdy wreath is shaped from wooden sticks instead of pine boughs.

What you need:

about twenty-four wooden tongue depressor sticks

white glue

green poster paint and a paintbrush

6-inch (15-cm) piece of green yarn

red ribbon or yarn

red beads or sequins

plastic wrap to work on

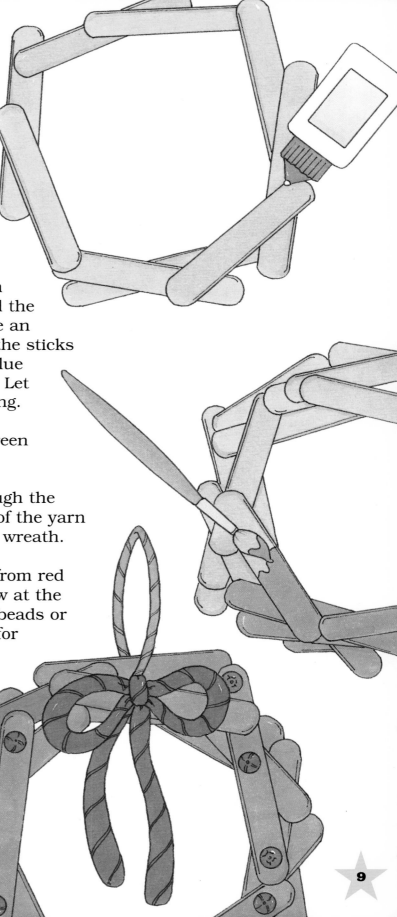

1 Tear off a piece of plastic wrap to cover your work surface. (Your wreath will not stick to the plastic wrap.)

2 Arrange the sticks in a wreath shape, layering them over each other as you build the circle shape. When you have an arrangement you like, glue the sticks to each other with dabs of glue at all the connecting points. Let the glue dry before continuing.

3 Paint the wreath with the green poster paint.

4 Thread the green yarn through the sticks and tie the two ends of the yarn together as a hanger for the wreath.

5 Make a bow for the wreath from red yarn or ribbon. Glue the bow at the top of the wreath. Glue red beads or sequins around the wreath for berries.

Once you have made the basic green wreath, you might have different ideas for decorating it.

Button Tree Magnet

These magnets are so easy to make that you can quickly make some to keep and some to give as gifts.

What you need:

lots of different buttons

green poster board

white glue

sparkle stem

scissors

sticky-back magnet

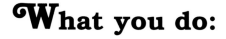

What you do:

1 Squeeze a glue outline of a Christmas tree, 3 inches (8 cm) high, on a piece of poster board. Fill the outline in with glue.

2 Sprinkle the glue with buttons to make a button tree. Do not put the buttons on flat. Overlap and stack them for a nice three-dimensional effect. Shape a tree with your fingers, adding more glue over the top buttons if needed.

3 When the glue has dried, cut the tree shape out.

4 Decorate the button tree by wrapping it with a sparkle stem to look like garland.

5 Press a strip of sticky-back magnet on the back of the tree.

Make lots of button trees to decorate your refrigerator. Think of other ways to decorate the trees. Try wrapping one in thin ribbon or sprinkling one with a layer of clear glitter.

Christmas Napkins

These decorative napkins add a festive touch to the holiday table.

What you need:

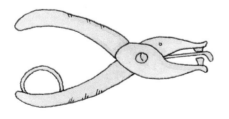

package
of red and
a package of
green napkins of
similar size

gold sticker stars

green yarn

small hole punch

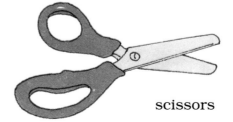

scissors

What you do:

1 Using a red paper napkin, folded as it comes in the package, cut a triangle Christmas tree shape at the point of the two bordered sides. This can be done quite easily by folding the napkin in half and cutting half a tree design at the fold.

2 Open up the napkin so that you can see the cut tree shape at all four corners of the napkin. Open up a green napkin and put the red napkin on top of the green one, so that the green napkin shows through the cut trees and around the edge of the red one if it is slightly larger (although it doesn't need to be). Arrange the napkins so that the folds of the two match exactly. Fold the two layers of the napkin back into quarters.

3 Fold the napkins in half again at the point, just the way you did when you cut the tree shape. Punch a hole below the tree shape through all the layers.

4 Open the napkin up again. Cut four 6-inch (15-cm) pieces of yarn. Thread a piece of yarn through the two holes punched below each tree and tie the yarn in a bow below the tree.

5 Tie the two napkins together at all four corners and top each tree with a gold star. Fold the napkin back up again.

Make a pretty holiday napkin for each person at your holiday table.

13

Holly Christmas Card Line

Hang all those pretty Christmas cards up for everyone to enjoy.

⭐hat you need:

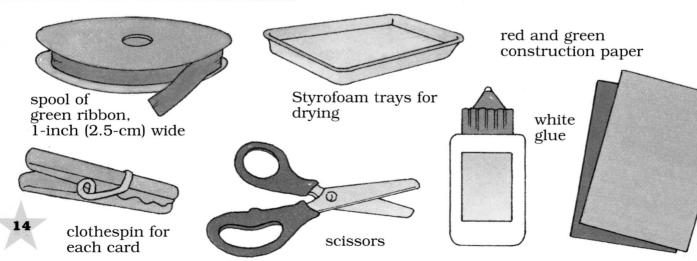

spool of
green ribbon,
1-inch (2.5-cm) wide

Styrofoam trays for
drying

red and green
construction paper

white
glue

clothespin for
each card

scissors

What you do:

1 Cut a 4-inch (10-cm) holly leaf from the green paper for each clothespin you are decorating. Glue a leaf to one side of each clothespin.

2 Cut three small berries from the red paper for each holly leaf. Glue the berries to the bottom of the holly leaf, at the clamp end of each clothespin. Let the clothespins dry on the Styrofoam tray.

3 Cut a length of green ribbon slightly longer than you want your card display to be. Tie each end of the ribbon to a secure place such as a curtain rod. Use a holly-covered clothespin to hang up each Christmas card you receive.

This is a decoration that gets prettier and prettier as you add more cards to it each day until Christmas.

Table Manger

This little table manger is a charming reminder of what Christmas is all about.

What you need:

fourteen craft sticks

blue felt

1-inch (2.5-cm) pom-pom in skin shade of your choice

white glue

craft moss

brown poster paint and a paintbrush

two wiggle eyes

yarn bits for hair

clamp clothespin

black and yellow pipe cleaners

scissors

Styrofoam tray to work on

modeling clay

What you do:

1 Glue two sticks into an X shape so that the bottom ends are about 2½ inches (6.5 cm) apart and the top ends are about 3½ inches (9 cm) apart. Glue a second pair of sticks in an X shape that is identical to the first pair of sticks. Do this by placing one pair of sticks on top of the other to make sure the match is exact. These will form the base for the manger.

2 It will be easier to glue the liner sticks in the manger if you use modeling clay to hold the two bases upright while you glue the five sticks across each side. Once the glue has dried, the manger can be removed from the clay and will stand on its own.

3 Paint the manger brown and let it dry.

4 Glue some craft moss in the manger to look like hay.

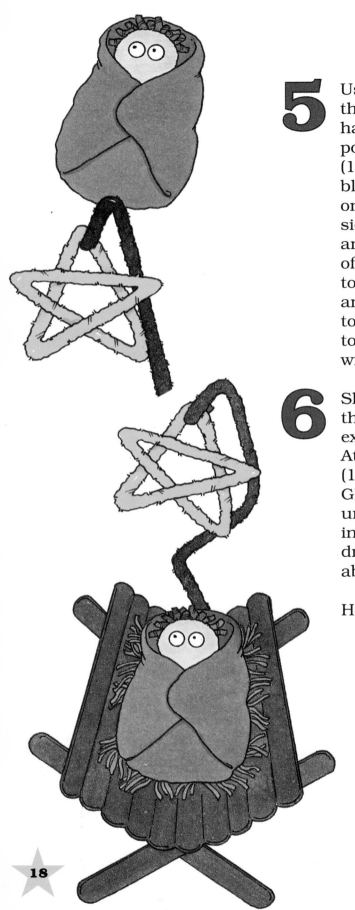

5 Use the pom-pom to make the head of the baby, gluing on some yarn bits for hair. Glue the two wiggle eyes on the pom-pom below the hair. Cut a 4-inch (10-cm) square from the blue felt for a blanket for the baby. Glue the head on one point of the square. Fold the two side points of the square to the center and glue them in place under the chin of the baby. Fold the bottom point up to meet the side folds of the blanket and glue it in place. Use the clothespin to hold the folds of the felt blanket together until the glue is dry. Glue the wrapped baby in the manger.

6 Shape a small star for the baby from the yellow pipe cleaner. Trim off any extra pipe cleaner you do not need. Attach the star to one end of a 6-inch (15-cm) piece of black pipe cleaner. Glue the other end of the pipe cleaner under the moss at the head of the baby in the manger. When the glue has dried, arrange the star so that it hangs above the head of the baby.

Happy Birthday, baby Jesus!

Cone Christmas Tree

Make this miniature version of a Christmas tree to display on a table—or on your head!

What you need:

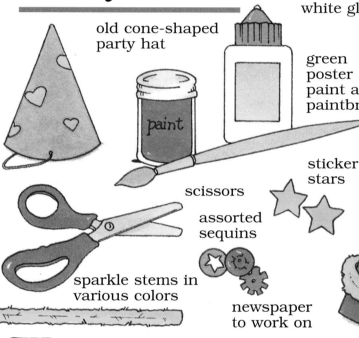

old cone-shaped party hat

white glue

green poster paint and a paintbrush

sticker stars

scissors

assorted sequins

sparkle stems in various colors

newspaper to work on

paint

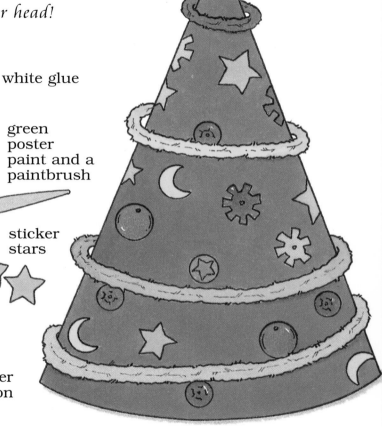

What you do:

1 Paint the hat green and let it dry.

2 Decorate the tree hat by gluing the sequins and sticker stars all over it.

3 Make circles of garland for the tree using different color sparkle stems.

Make each circle slightly smaller so that each one rests on the tree at a different height.

If you are making more than one tree to use as hats at a Christmas party, you might want to just paint the hats green and leave the fun of decorating to your guests.

Santa Tissue Box

Turn a tissue box into a cheerful Santa for the holidays.

What you need:

square shaped tissue box with tissue still in it

fiberfill or cotton balls

red, white, black, and pink construction paper

white glue

scissors

What you do:

1 Turn the box on its side and pull the first tissue partway out to form the beard for the Santa.

2 Cut a triangle-shaped hat from the red construction paper and glue it to the edge of the box above the beard.

3 Cut cheeks from the pink paper, eyes from the black and the white paper, and a nose from the red paper. Glue the facial features on the space between the beard and the hat.

4 Use the fiberfill or cotton balls to make hair on each side of the face and fur trim for the bottom edge and top tip of the hat.

Tissue box Santas make delightful and useful gifts for the holiday season.

Soft-Sculpture Snowman

This happy and huggable snowman wants to decorate your room this Christmas season.

What you need:

adult large-size
white T-shirt

big red
pom-pom

colorful old
adult-size sock

fabric scrap

red, green, black,
and orange felt

four sturdy
rubber bands

bag of
fiberfill

white
glue

scissors

What you do:

1 Push the sleeves to the inside of the shirt. Gather the fabric around the neck opening and hold it together with a rubber band. Stuff the top part of the shirt with fiberfill for the head of the snowman. Use a rubber band to hold the head stuffing in place and form the neck.

2 Stuff the bottom of the shirt with fiberfill. Close the bottom of the snowman with a rubber band.

3 Cut the cuff off the colorful sock to make a hat for the snowman. Pull the cuff down over the gathered neck of the shirt at the top of the snowman. Glue the cuff hat in place. Roll the bottom edge of the cuff up to form the brim of the hat. Close the top of the cuff with a rubber band. Glue the red pom-pom at the top of the hat.

4 Use the fabric scrap to cut a scarf for the snowman, and tie it around his neck.

5 Cut a carrot nose for the snowman from the orange felt. Cut circles of black felt for the eyes, mouth, and buttons of the snowman. Glue the face pieces and buttons on the snowman.

6 Give the snowman a Christmasy look by cutting two holly leaves from the green felt and some holly berries from the red felt. Glue the holly on one side of the snowman.

This snowman will not melt, even when you give him a Christmas hug!

Christmas Stocking Pencil Holder

Make this project to decorate your desk for the holidays.

What you need:

toddler-size red sock

cardboard toilet-tissue tube

fiberfill

two red sequins

white glue

green felt scrap

scissors

What you do:

1 Stuff the foot of the sock with fiberfill to give it shape.

2 Slide the cardboard tube straight down into the cuff of the sock, so that the end is in the heel, with all the fiberfill pushed to one side into the foot of the sock.

3 Rub glue around the top inside of the tube. Fold the top of the sock cuff down into the glue-covered rim of the tube. Let the glue dry to hold the tube in place inside the sock.

4 Cut two holly leaves from the green felt. Glue the leaves at the top of the stocking holder. Glue the sequins between the leaves for berries.

You can make this pencil holder using any Christmasy socks and trims that you might have on hand.

Shelf Elf

Make this little elf to sit on the edge of your shelf or mantel.

What you need:

cereal box

cellophane tape

jingle bell

pencil

red and white pipe cleaners

red rickrack

two wiggle eyes

fiberfill

white glue

green and pink construction paper

small red and large green pom-poms

scissors

What you do:

1 Starting at one corner of the bottom of the box, cut a triangle shaped corner from the box with the cut side of the triangle being about as long as the bottom of the box.

2 Cover the front, back, and sides of the box with green paper. Do this by tracing around each side of the box with a pencil and cutting out each resulting shape to glue over the side you traced.

3 Cut a round face from the pink construction paper. Glue it to one side of the box about 1½ inches (4 cm) below the point at the top of the triangle.

4 Glue a strip of rickrack across the top of the head to form the bottom of a pointed hat for the elf. Glue the large green pom-pom to the top of the hat.

5 Glue the two wiggle eyes and the red pom-pom nose to the face. Glue fiberfill around the face for hair and a beard.

6 Glue a strip of rickrack across the bottom of the box.

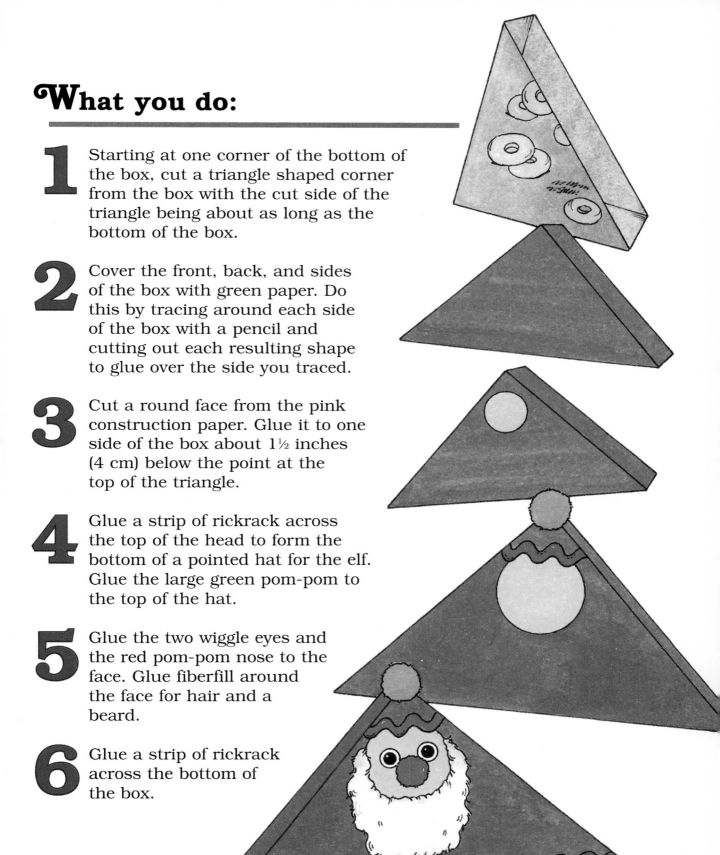

7 Tape the ends of two 12-inch (30-cm) pipe cleaners to the inside front of the box so that they hang down to form legs. Bend the legs forward, then down, to form knees so that the elf can sit with the legs hanging over the edge of a shelf or mantel. Bend the end of each leg forward to make feet.

8 Poke a hole about halfway down each side of the elf. Slip the end of a 6-inch (15-cm) piece of pipe cleaner through each hole to make arms. Tape the ends of the pipe cleaners to the inside of the box elf to hold them in place.

9 Twist 5-inch (13-cm) pieces of red and white pipe cleaner together to make a candy cane for the elf to hold in one hand. Wrap the end of one pipe-cleaner arm around the candy cane to hold it. Slip the jingle bell over the end of the other hand.

Do you hear a bell ringing?

Jingle Bell Napkin Rings

This project looks and sounds like Christmas!

What you need:

6-inch (15-cm) red pipe cleaner for each ring

 nine jingle bells for each ring

 nine red craft beads for each ring

What you do:

1 String the beads and the jingle bells onto the pipe cleaner, alternating between the two. When they are all on the pipe cleaner, twist the two ends of the pipe cleaner together to form a ring.

You can make your napkin rings all the same or make lots of different ones. Try using different color beads and jingle bells of different sizes. You might even want to buy a package of pretty Christmas napkins and match your pipe cleaner and bead colors to the napkins you chose.

Cone Table Santa

Turn an old party hat into jolly old St. Nick!

What you need:

old cone-shaped
party hat

red poster paint and
a paintbrush

red and
white
pipe
cleaners

green ribbon, ¼-inch
(.5 cm) wide

two
wiggle
eyes

white
glue

red, green, and pink
construction paper

scissors

small red
pom-pom

newspaper to
work on

fiberfill

What you do:

1 Paint the entire outside of the party hat red.

2 Cut a 2½-inch (6-cm) circle from the pink paper for a face. Glue the face about 2 inches (5 cm) down from the point of the hat.

3 Glue a band of fiberfill all the way around the hat just above the face to form the base of the Santa hat. Glue a ball of fiberfill at the point of the hat.

4 Glue fiberfill on both sides of the face for hair and along the bottom of the face for a beard.

5 Glue the two wiggle eyes on the face below the hat. Glue on the red pom-pom for a nose.

6 Glue the two ends of a strip of ribbon around the Santa for a belt.

7 Cut two arms from the red paper and two mittens from the green paper. Glue a mitten on the end of each arm and glue an arm on each side of the Santa. Glue fiberfill across the cuff of each arm to look like fur.

8 Twist two 2½-inch (6-cm) pieces of pipe cleaner, one red and one white, together to make a candy cane. Fold the mitten of one hand around the candy cane and glue it in place to look like Santa is holding the candy.

HO! HO! HO!
Merry Christmas!

Gift Picture Frame

What better gift than a picture of someone you love?

What you need:

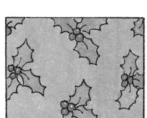
small cardboard box, such as a jewelry box

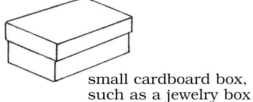
Christmas wrapping paper

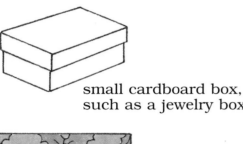
colored tissue paper that looks nice with the wrapping paper

scissors

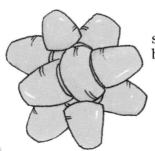
small package bow

cellophane tape

white glue

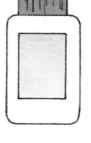
photograph

What you do:

1 Open the box and wrap the top and the bottom separately, folding the paper down to cover the inside edges of both the bottom and the lid.

2 Glue the bow to the top of the lid.

3 Rub glue all over the inside of the box bottom. Tuck in squares of colored tissue paper in the box so that it covers the bottom and sides of the box and sticks out around the edges like an opened package.

4 Glue a photo in the bottom of the box.

5 Glue the lid of the box at an angle across the top corner of the box bottom. When the glue has dried, stand the box up so that the package becomes a picture frame.

You don't have to wait until Christmas morning to peek inside this package!

33

Doorknob-Nose Elf

What an unusual nose!

What you need:

two uncoated 9-inch (23-cm) paper plates

garland

red, black, green, and white construction paper

rickrack

poster paint in the skin color of your choice and a paintbrush

pom-pom

red marker

scissors

white glue

newspaper to work on

What you do:

1 Glue the two paper plates together to make a stronger plate.

Cut a 4-inch (10-cm) slit across the center of the plate. Cut another 4-inch slit across that slit to form an X-shaped opening that will be used to slip the plate over a doorknob.

3 Paint the bottom side (not the eating side) of the plate for the face of the elf.

4 Cut a piece of garland long enough to go three quarters of the way around the edge of the plate for a beard. Glue the garland beard in place.

5 Cut a triangle-shaped hat for the elf from the green paper. Glue the hat to the top of the elf's head. Decorate the hat with rickrack. Glue the pom-pom to the point of the hat.

6 Cut eyes from the white and black paper. Use the marker to draw a big, happy smile on the elf, then glue a round cheek on each side of the smile.

Give the elf a big shiny nose by slipping the plate over a doorknob.

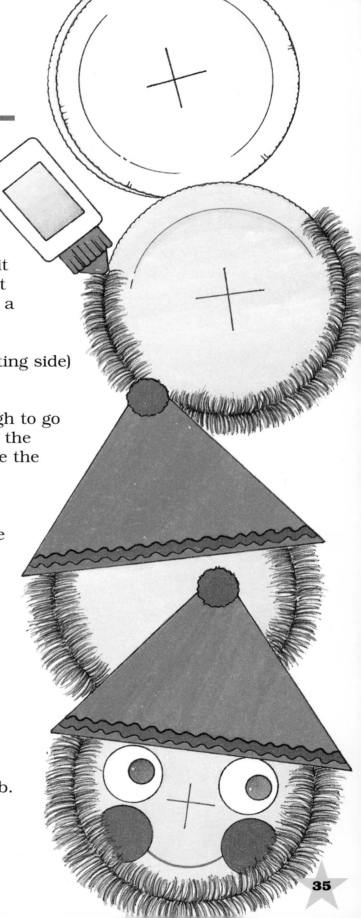

Foil Angel

Make this little angel to look just like you!

What you need:

heavy-duty aluminum foil

pencil

masking tape

white glue

pink and yellow construction paper

yarn in your hair color

yarn for a hanger

markers

sparkle stem

scissors

sticker stars

construction paper in skin color of your choice

What you do:

1 Tear off two squares of foil. Fold each square back and forth like a fan to pleat it. Squeeze one folded square of foil together at one end and fan out the other end to make the dress for the angel. Squeeze the other folded square of foil together in the middle and fan out each side for the arms of the dress.

2 Squeeze the neck of the dress and the center of the arms together to attach them. Use masking tape to help secure them together.

3 Cut a 6-inch (15-cm) piece of yarn. Tie the yarn around the neck of the dress, then tie the two ends together to make a hanger for the angel.

4 Cut a construction paper head for the angel. Glue yarn to the head in your hair style. Use the markers to draw a face. Cut heart shaped cheeks from the pink paper and glue them on the face.

5 Shape a halo from the sparkle stem. Use glue and masking tape to attach the stem of the halo to the back of the head.

6 Glue the head over the masking tape at the neck of the dress.

7 Use the pencil to trace your hands on the yellow paper. Cut out both hands. Glue the two hands sticking out from the back of the angel for wings. Place a piece of masking tape over the spot where you will be gluing the wings to create a better gluing surface.

8 Decorate your angel with the sticker stars.

Hang this angel up to remind your favorite grownups how good you've been this year!

37

Stacked Package Christmas Tree

This centerpiece is the perfect project to do as a group to take to a hospital or nursing home during the Christmas season.

What you need:

twenty small empty gelatin or pudding boxes

Christmas wrap in several different patterns

package bow

white glue

cellophane tape

glitter

plastic trash bag to work on

scissors

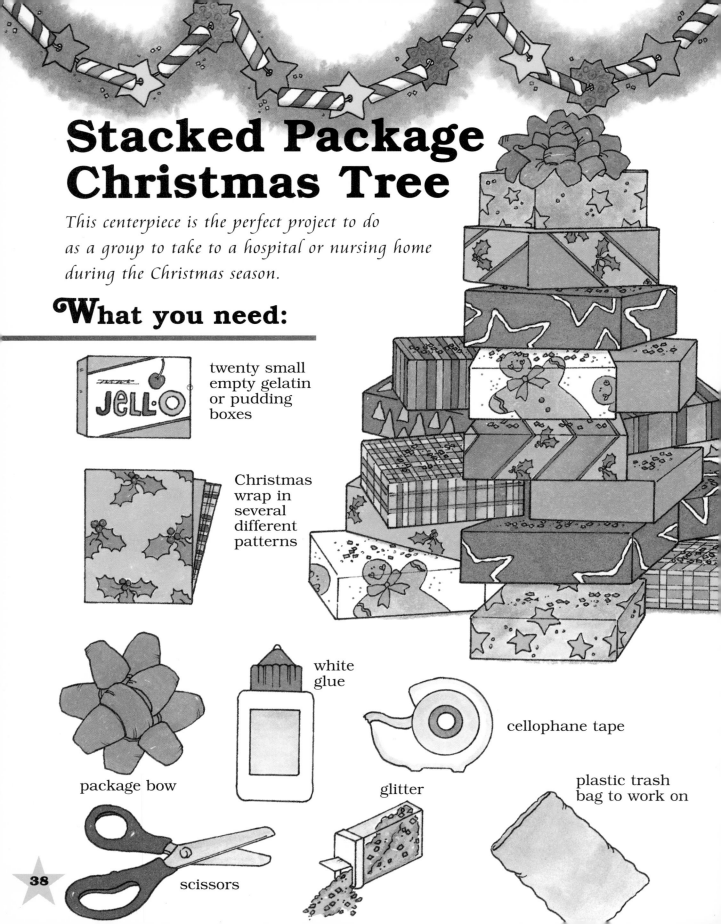

What you do:

1 Close the open end of each box and tape it shut. Wrap each box in Christmas wrap, using a variety of different wraps.

2 Stack the boxes on the plastic bag in a tree shape. Start with four boxes on the bottom, then angle three boxes on top of those, three more layers of three boxes, then two boxes, then two layers of one box. When you are satisfied with the arrangement of the boxes, glue them all together.

3 Dab glue on the exposed areas of the boxes and sprinkle the tree with glitter.

4 Top the package tree by gluing the bow on the top box.

If you are doing this with a group, divide the number of boxes needed by the number of people helping, and ask each person to bring in an assigned number of wrapped boxes. This will give the tree lots of different wrapping paper patterns.

Christmas Memories Box

This project is just what you need to store all those wonderful Christmas memories.

What you need:

shoe box with a lid

five large zip-to-close bags

Christmas wrapping paper

scissors

stapler

markers

white glue

cellophane tape

construction paper in Christmas colors

What you do:

1 Wrap the lid and the bottom of the box separately in the Christmas wrap.

2 Cut a piece of construction paper to fit inside each of the plastic bags. Line each bag.

3 Cut a piece of paper to fit in the bottom of the box. Staple the paper to the side of one bag, stapling only the back of the bag, behind the liner. Also, staple the paper along the bottom edge of the bag, through both sides of the bag.

4 Staple the side of the next bag to the side of the first bag, making sure that the openings face in the same direction. Staple all the bags together to form a strip of five bags.

5 Cut a piece of paper to fit in the lid of the shoe box. Staple the piece to the side of the last bag in the row, stapling behind the liner. Also, staple the paper along the bottom edge of the bag, through both sides of the bag.

6 Glue the back paper on one end of the row of bags onto the bottom of the box. Glue the back paper on the other end of the row of bags onto the lid of the shoe box. Let the glue dry.

7 Cut Christmas shapes to glue on the lid of the box. Label the box with your name and the year.

Use tape to attach favorite cards, photos, and small favors to the paper liners in the bags. To display your collection, pull the lid out from the box. When Christmas is over, fold your memories back into the box.

heather's memories 1998 christmas

Three Kings

Make three kings in different color combinations to create a beautiful holiday display.

What you need for each king:

yellow plastic cup

colorful tissue paper

small salad dressing bottle

construction paper in skin tone of your choice

paper towel

white glue

scissors

masking tape

trims

yarn in hair and beard colors of your choice

markers in black and skin tones of your choice

sparkle stem

newspaper to work on

sparkling clip-on earring

What you do for each king:

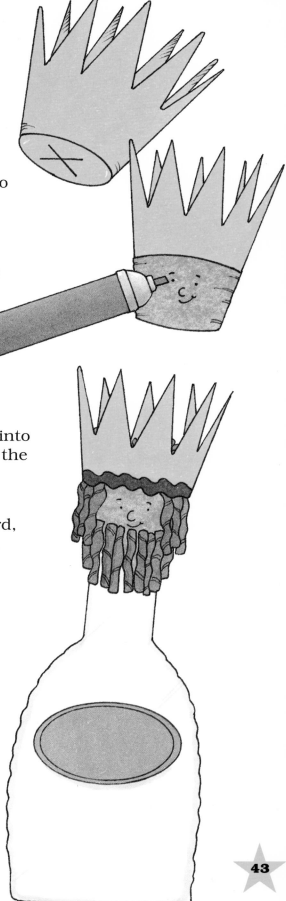

1 Cut the top third of the yellow cup into points to look like a crown. Cut an X shape in the bottom of the cup.

2 Wrap the portion of the cup under the crown with masking tape for the face. Use a marker to color the face area masking tape in the skin tone of your choice. Use a black marker to draw on a face.

3 Stuff a crumpled piece of paper towel into the crown. It will cover the opening of the bottle.

4 Glue yarn bits onto the face for a beard, and over the paper towel in the crown and around the face for hair.

5 Glue a strip of trim around the bottom of the crown.

6 Slide the bottom of the cup over the neck of the bottle.

7 Wrap the bottle in a double layer of tissue paper for a robe. Secure the robe around the neck of the bottle with the sparkle stem. Glue the top of the robe to cover the back of the head.

8 Cut hands from construction paper in a shade to match the face. Glue the hands to the front of the robe. Clip the jeweled earring between the two hands to look like a gift.

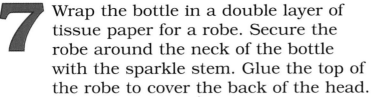

"We three kings from Orient are . . ."

Christmas Light Catcher

This simple project fascinates everyone who sees it.

What you need:

scissors

small baby food jar

gold star sequins

thin red ribbon

craft stick

clear hair gel

red sequins

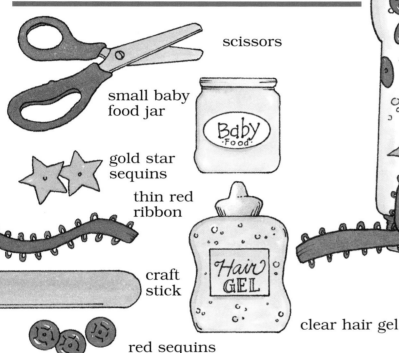

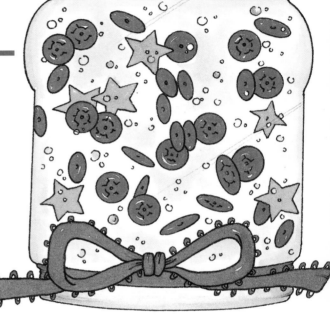

What you do:

1 Remove the label from the jar. Make sure the jar and lid are clean.

2 Fill the jar with clear hair gel.

3 Put about 100 sequins and stars in the gel. Use the craft stick to mix them into the gel.

4 Put the lid on the jar. Tie a piece of red ribbon around the rim of the lid in a bow. Stand the jar on its lid in a sunny window.

You can use any color or shape sequins you wish for this project, then match the ribbon to the sequins you choose. You might also want to try making one with pearls or other small beads.

45

Glistening Snowman

This sparkling snowman will last for many holidays to come.

What you need:

spaghetti

1-lb spaghetti box

cotton batting

buttons

orange pipe cleaner

fabric scrap

yarn

masking tape

colorful old adult-size sock

clear glitter

white glue

scissors

hairspray

newspaper to work on

What you do:

1 Cover the box with a sheet of cotton batting and glue it in place.

2 Spray the cotton batting with hairspray, then quickly sprinkle it with glitter. You may need an adult to help you with this part.

3 Cut the cuff from the sock. Tie one end of the cuff closed with a piece of yarn. Tie the yarn into a bow. Rub glue all over the top end of the box and slip the cuff over the glue to put a hat on the snowman. Fold the bottom of the sock hat up to make a brim.

4 Tie a long strip of fabric around the box to make a scarf for the snowman.

5 Glue on buttons for the eyes, mouth, and buttons. To give each button a better gluing surface, put a piece of masking tape on the back before gluing it to the snowman.

6 Wrap an orange pipe cleaner into a spiral to make a carrot nose for the snowman. Trim off any extra pipe cleaner when the nose looks long enough. Glue the nose in place on the snowman.

You might want to add other decorations to the snowman, such as a jingle bell tied to the hat or cut-out felt shapes glued on the end of the scarf.

47

Giant Star

Make this bright and shining giant star to remind you of the one that shone over the baby Jesus on the night he was born.

What you need:

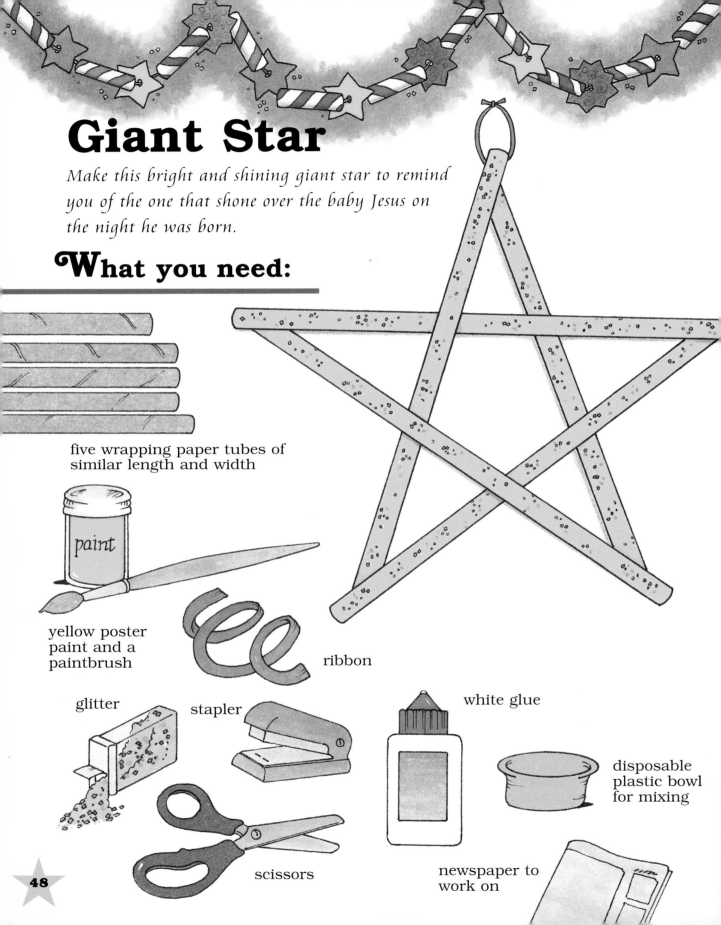

five wrapping paper tubes of similar length and width

yellow poster paint and a paintbrush

ribbon

glitter

stapler

white glue

disposable plastic bowl for mixing

scissors

newspaper to work on

What you do:

1 Assemble the tubes in the shape of a star in the same pattern you would use if you were drawing a star on paper without lifting your pencil. Flatten the ends of the tubes at each contact point that is a tip of the star and staple the ends together.

2 Mix one part white glue with four parts yellow paint in the plastic bowl. Paint the star with the paint and glue mixture, then immediately sprinkle the star with glitter.

3 Cut a piece of ribbon 12 inches (30 cm) long. String one end of the ribbon through the opening of one of the points of the star and tie the two ends together to make a hanger.

Twinkle, twinkle, great big star!

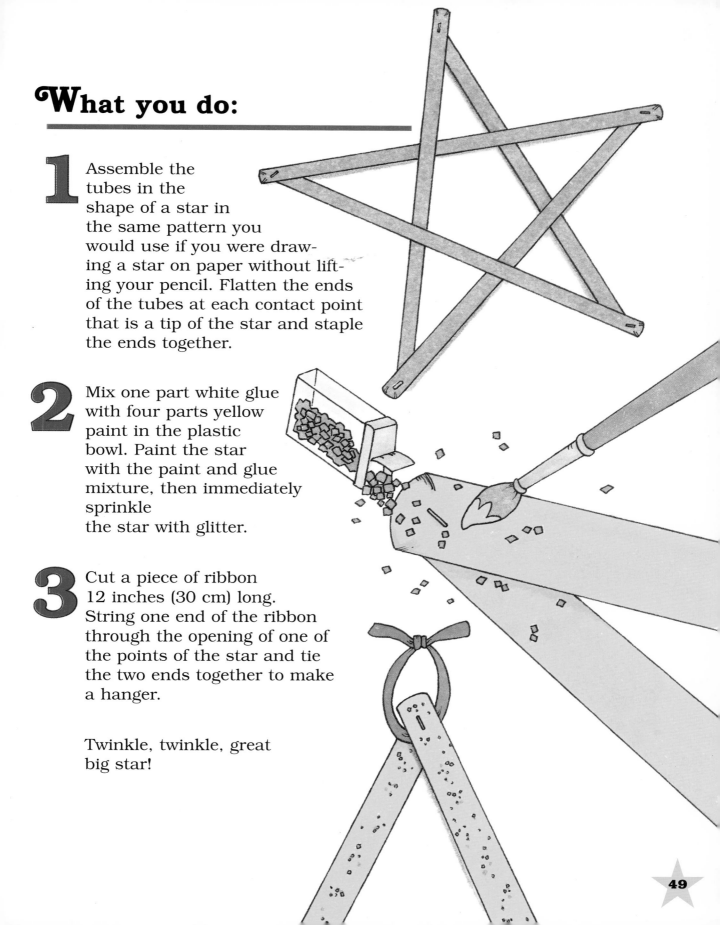

Christmas Carolers

The cluster of carolers makes a charming Christmas decoration.

What you need:

two cardboard paper-towel tubes

two cardboard toilet-tissue tubes

red, green, and white construction paper

Christmas print wrapping paper

cellophane tape

white glue

scissors

rubber band

markers

heavy yarn or fabric scraps

yarn

two colorful child-size socks

two colorful adult-size socks

construction paper in the skin tones of your choice

What you do:

1 Cut one of the two long tubes so that it is an inch or two shorter than the other tube.

2 Cover all four tubes with a different paper, using the wrapping paper and the red and green construction paper. Glue the paper around each tube and hold it in place with cellophane tape.

3 Wrap the top part of each tube with a strip of skin-colored construction paper, gluing it, then securing it with tape.

4 Cut the cuff off each of the four socks to make hats for the carolers. Tie the open end of each cuff closed with a piece of colorful yarn tied in a bow. Glue the cuff hats from the adult socks on the tall tube carolers and the cuff hats from the children's socks on the short tube carolers.

5 Use the markers to draw a face on each caroler.

6 Tie a piece of heavy yarn or a fabric scrap around the neck of each caroler for a scarf.

7 Glue the two tall carolers together side by side. Glue the two short carolers together side by side and in front of the tall carolers. Use a rubber band to hold the carolers together until the glue dries.

8 Cut a music book for each pair of carolers from the white paper. Decorate each book by using the markers. Glue a book in front of each pair of carolers.

"Joy to the world . . ."

Gift-Wrapped Bathroom Tissue Cover

Even the bathroom can take on a festive look with this useful holiday craft.

What you need:

wrapped single roll of toilet tissue

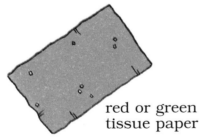
red or green tissue paper

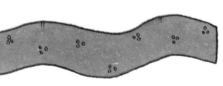
ribbon

large oatmeal box

scissors

white glue

What you do:

1 Cut the top half of the oatmeal box off, making sure the remaining bottom portion is taller than the roll of toilet tissue. Slide the roll into the bottom of the oatmeal box and trim around the edge of the box so that it exactly fits over the roll.

2 Cut a double-thickness square of tissue paper that is large enough to cover the bottom and the sides of the box.

3 Remove the roll, and rub glue all the way around the inside rim of the box. Turn the box over and place the center of the tissue square over the bottom of the box. Smooth the tissue down, evenly pleating it around the sides of the box. Trim off any large extra pieces of tissue paper and tuck the ends into the box, pressing the roll of toilet tissue way into the box to hold the tissue in place while the glue dries. If you have a lot of drippy glue inside the box, you might want to cover the roll of toilet tissue with a piece of plastic wrap first to keep it clean and to prevent gluing it inside the box. When the glue has dried, remove the roll, take off the plastic wrap, and slide the roll back into the cover.

4 Tie a pretty ribbon around the tissue roll cover and tie it in a bow.

What a pretty way to hide that extra roll!

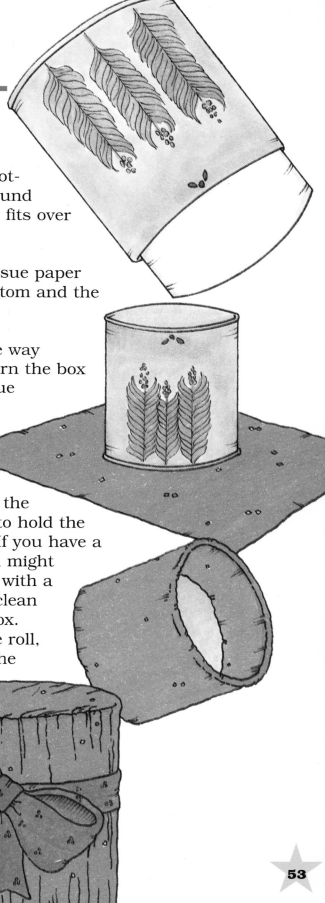

Tube Reindeer

When you finish your holiday wrapping, you can use the empty tubes to make a reindeer.

What you need:

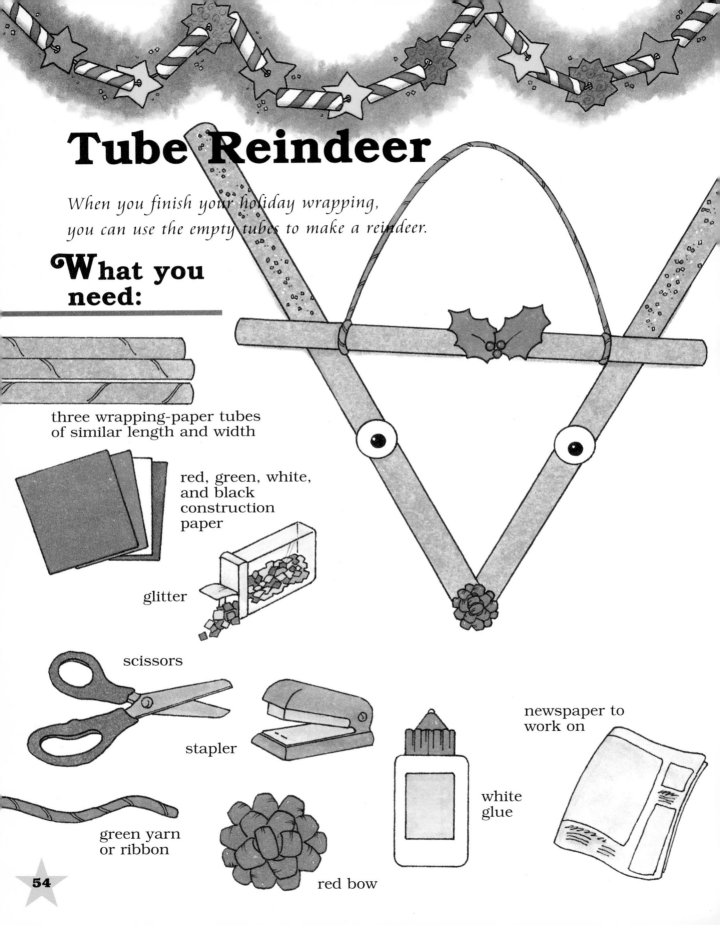

three wrapping-paper tubes of similar length and width

red, green, white, and black construction paper

glitter

scissors

stapler

newspaper to work on

white glue

green yarn or ribbon

red bow

What you do:

1 Flatten the ends of two tubes and staple them together in a V-shape.

2 Glue the third tube across the middle of the V so that it forms ears and the top half of the V forms antlers.

3 Cut eyes for the reindeer from the black and white paper. Glue an eye to the center of each tube below the ears.

4 Glue the red bow to the point of the V for a red nose.

5 Cut holly leaves from the green paper and berries from the red paper. Glue the holly and berries between the two ears.

6 Rub glue on the antlers and sprinkle them with glitter.

7 Cut a 3-foot (90-cm) length of ribbon or yarn. Tie one end to each ear of the reindeer to make a hanger.

Does the red nose make you think of a very famous reindeer?

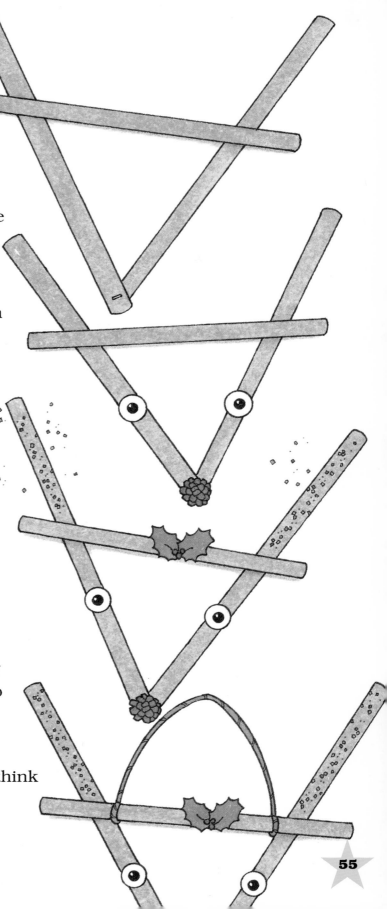

Snack Bag Angel

For this project, you'll need to look for the silver lining.

What you need:

two snack bags (popcorn or potato chips) that are lined in silver

chips

construction paper in the skin color of your choice

rubber band

gold garland

bits of yarn in hair color of your choice

markers

scissors

masking tape

white glue

blue plastic wrap

PLASTIC WRAP

plastic grocery bags for stuffing

What you do:

1 Turn both bags inside out and wash them in soapy water. Let the bags dry before continuing.

2 Stuff one bag lightly with plastic grocery bags. Twist the top closed and secure it with masking tape.

3 Tear off a sheet of blue plastic wrap long enough to drape over the top of the bag and cover the front and back with a layer of blue. Squeeze the wrap around the stem at the top of the bag. Secure it with masking tape.

4 Gather the second bag together at the center to make wings. Attach the wings to the stem of the first bag with the rubber band.

5 Cut a head for the angel from construction paper. Use the markers to give the angel a face. Glue on bits of yarn for hair. Wrap a halo of gold garland around the top of the head and secure it at the back of the head with glue and masking tape.

6 Glue the head to the masking tape–wrapped stem of the dress.

With a little arranging, this angel will stand without additional support.

Triangle Santa

This jumbo Santa Claus looks great hanging on a door.

What you need:

large sheet of red poster board

large red pom-pom

scissors

pink, black, white, yellow, and skin-color construction paper

white glue

fiberfill

58

What you do:

1 Cut as large a triangle as you can from the poster board with the bottom of the triangle shorter than the two sides.

2 Cut an 8-inch (20-cm) circle from the skin-colored paper for a face. Glue the face about 6 inches (15 cm) below the point of the triangle.

3 Glue a line of fiberfill across the top of the head to define the bottom of the hat. Glue a ball of fiberfill at the point of the hat.

4 Cut eyes from the white and black paper. Glue the eyes on the face below the hat. Cut cheeks from the pink paper. Glue them to the face below the eyes.

5 Glue fiberfill to the head for hair and a beard. Glue the pom-pom above the beard for a nose.

6 Cut a belt from black paper. Glue the belt across the middle of the triangle. Trim the edges to make it fit exactly. Cut a belt buckle from the yellow paper. Glue the buckle to the middle of the belt.

7 Cut two boots for Santa from the black paper. Glue the top of each boot to the bottom back of the triangle so that they hang down from the triangle Santa. Glue a line of fiberfill across each boot to look like fur.

HO! HO! HO!

Reindeer Treat Box

*This reindeer is the perfect container
for storing or delivering a batch of Christmas cookies.*

What you need:

brown,
black, and white
construction
paper

round oatmeal
box with lid

scissors

masking
tape

white glue

two 12-inch (30-cm)
brown pipe cleaners

heavy red
yarn or ribbon

red
pom-pom

red rickrack

red tissue paper

What you do:

1 Cover the outside of the box and the lid with strips of masking tape to create a better gluing surface. Cover the box and the lid with brown construction paper.

2 Cut two ears from the brown paper and glue them to the sides of the box.

3 Make eyes from the black and white paper. Glue the eyes to the box just below the ears.

4 Glue the red pom-pom to the box below the eyes for a nose.

5 Poke a hole through each side of the box just behind the ears. Make each antler by cutting a 3-inch (8-cm) piece of pipe cleaner and wrapping it around the rest of the pipe cleaner towards one end to form the branches of the antler. Slide the end of a pipe cleaner antler into each hole and use masking tape to secure the end of the pipe cleaner inside the box.

6 Tie the red yarn or ribbon in a bow around the neck of the reindeer.

7 Trim the bottom of the box by gluing a strip of red rickrack around it.

8 Line the inside of the box with a square of red tissue and you are ready to tuck in a batch of Christmas cookies to deliver to a friend or neighbor.

Yum!

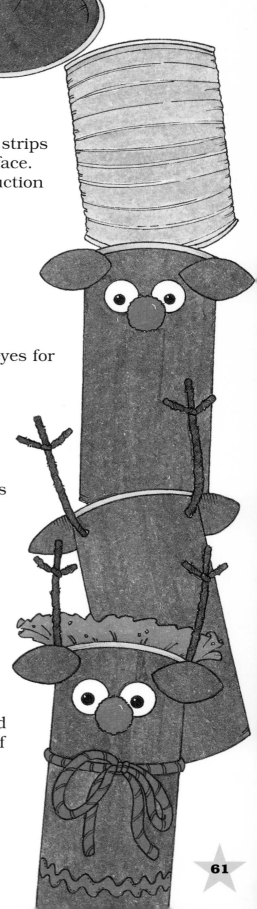

Noel Picture Frame

The French word for Christmas is Noël.

What you need:

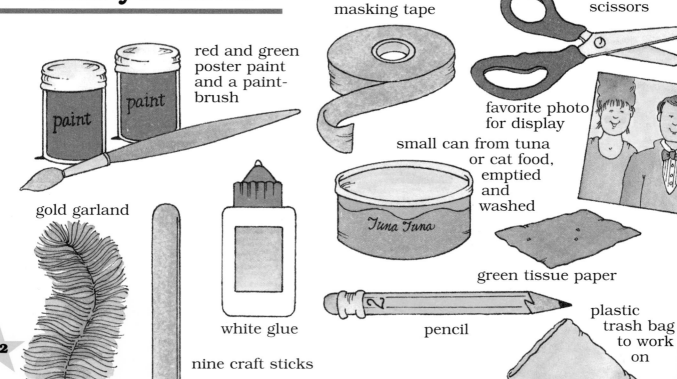

red and green poster paint and a paintbrush

masking tape

scissors

favorite photo for display

small can from tuna or cat food, emptied and washed

green tissue paper

gold garland

white glue

pencil

plastic trash bag to work on

nine craft sticks

What you do:

1 Glue the sticks together to make an N, E, and L. The tuna can will be the letter O.

2 Paint the stick letters and let them dry on the plastic trash bag.

3 Center the can on the photo. Use the pencil to trace around the can on the photo. Cut out the photo on the traced line.

4 Cover all surfaces of the can, inside and out, with strips of masking tape to create a better gluing surface. Cut a double thickness of green tissue paper large enough to press inside the can to cover it, then wrap down over the sides of the can to cover to the back of the can. Glue the tissue in place to cover the can.

5 Press the photo into the bottom of the can. Use a small dab of glue behind the photo if you need to.

6 Glue two rows of gold garland around the outside of the can.

7 Glue the N to the left side of the can and the E and L on the right side of the can to spell NOEL. Let the project dry face down on the plastic trash bag.

Noel, Noel!

About the Author
and Illustrator

Twenty-five years as a teacher and director of nursery school programs has given Kathy Ross extensive experience in guiding young children through crafts projects. Among the more than 30 craft books she has written are *Gifts to Make for Your Favorite Grownup, Crafts From Your Favorite Fairy Tales,* and the *Crafts for All Seasons* series.

Sharon Lane Holm, a resident of Fairfield, Connecticut, won awards for her work in advertising design before shifting her concentration to children's books. Among the books she has illustrated recently are *Sidewalk Games Around the World* and *Happy Birthday, Everywhere!,* both by Arlene Erlbach, and *Beautiful Bats* by Linda Glaser.

Together, Kathy Ross and Sharon Lane Holm have also created the popular *Holiday Crafts for Kids* series as well as the *Crafts for Kids Who Are Wild About* series.